JESUS' LOVE STORIES

Scriptural Insights into the Spirituality of Christian Loving

John F. Loya
Joseph A. Loya, OSA

Paulist Press
New York/Mahwah, N.J.

Nihil Obstat: The Reverend John G. Vrana
                Censor Deputatus

Imprimatur: The Most Reverend Richard G. Lennon, M. Th., M.A.
               Bishop of Cleveland

Given at Cleveland, Ohio on 31 July 2006

The *Nihil Obstat* and *Imprimatur* are official declarations that a book or pamphlet is free of doctrinal or moral error. No implication is contained therein that those who have granted the *Nihil Obstat* and *Imprimatur* agree with the contents, opinions, or statements expressed.

The scripture quotations contained herein are from the New Revised Standard Version: Catholic Edition Copyright © 1989 and 1993, by the Division of Christian Education of the National Council of the Churches of Christ in the United States of America. Used by permission. All rights reserved.

Cover design by Cynthia Dunne

Library of Congress Cataloging-in-Publication Data

Loya, John F.
   Jesus' love stories : scriptural insights into the spirituality of
   Christian loving / John F. Loya, Joseph A. Loya.
   p. cm. — (IlluminationBooks)
   Includes bibliographical references.
   ISBN 978-0-8091-4439-6 (alk. paper)
   1. Love—Biblical teaching. 2. Jesus Christ—Parables. I. Loya, Joseph A.
II. Title.
   BS2545.L6L69 2007
   241'.4—dc22

                                                    2007003048

Published by Paulist Press
997 Macarthur Boulevard
Mahwah, New Jersey 07430

www.paulistpress.com

Printed and bound in the United States of America

Contents

Acknowledgments

My brother and I would like to acknowledge and express our gratitude to Kathy Simmons, Lori Eppich, Bertha Popovic, Rev. John G. Vrana, and Kevin Carrizo di Camillo for their help in bringing this book to print. Their technical support, insightful comments, and creative suggestions contributed greatly toward shaping and fashioning the narrative of these pages. If this book should bear any fruit for the reader, these people had no small part in this work of love.

Dedication

We dedicate this book to our parents,
Joseph and Anna Marie,
our first and best teachers in the ways of faith and love.

Prologue

The book you hold in your hands is authored by two ordained Catholic "preachers." The following section begins with an anecdote about preaching that leads to a "how to" type question about the most profound of human experiences— love. But this question is presupposed by the more fundamental question of "why": specifically, why a book on love by a couple of preachers? Our response is rooted in the very essence and object of preaching, which is to communicate through words the power of the living Word of God—the Word of Love—so as to inspire free submission to this power that creates, transforms, heals, and saves us all.

The fundamental source text of preaching is, of course, holy scripture. The entire Bible can be thought of as a divine marriage proposal. The prophets of Israel bear witness to this special bond for which we were made:

> For your Maker is your husband, the LORD of hosts is his name; the Holy One of Israel is your Redeemer, the God of the whole earth he is called....For the mountains may depart and the hills be removed, but my steadfast love shall not depart from you, and my covenant of peace shall not be removed, says the LORD, who has compassion on you.
>
> (Isa 54:5, 10)

This great matrimonial mystery is fulfilled in the new covenant that Christ the redeemer established with his bride-church (see Eph 5:21–33). The entire Christian life bears the mark of the spousal love of Christ and the church. "Already Baptism, the entry into the People of God, is a nuptial mystery; it is so to speak the nuptial bath which precedes the wedding feast, the Eucharist," instructs the *Catechism of the Catholic Church*.[1] The sacred scriptures that began with the creation of man and woman through and for love in the image and likeness of God conclude with the author of the Book of Revelation envisioning a culminating consummation at the fulfillment of history.

Proclamation of the word of love is especially needed in these times in which the world is at once getting "smaller" and becoming ever more polarized and conflict-ridden. World cultures are diverging and are becoming ever more specialized, segmented, segregated, unequal, and hyperopposed. Editorialist David Brooks has noted that it was not long ago that social observers speculated with confidence and enthusiasm about globalization and the revolution in communications technology bringing us all together, but just the opposite is proving to be true.[2] Fear, which is the opposite of love, abounds. It is fear that spontaneously spawns the furies of anger, bigotry, hatred, and aggression. The extreme multiplicity of meanings ascribed to love in contemporary culture is not serving such a world well in terms of promoting unity, stability, reconciliation, and peace that are to mark the fully revealed reign of the Lord to come. Frenetic and pressure-filled scrambles to be fulfilled by kinds of loving that cannot fulfill because they are devoid of saving power often bring their own exasperations and anguished sense of loss. Those stories can be heard every day.

To hear of love as it is written about in the sacred scriptures, the love taught by the one hailed as Wonderful Counselor, Mighty God, Prince of Peace (see Isa 9:6), and to be open to its powers, requires a proper understanding of its particular sense. To convey that understanding is the purpose of this effort. No more, no less.

Two concluding points regarding the intentions of this book: Following Pope John Paul II's prayer that the church of Christ may breathe with two lungs—the religious genius of the (Latin) West and the (Greek) East—a conscious effort has been made by the authors to draw from the rich spiritual and theological depositories of both great traditions.[3] Also, the annotated list of recommended readings provided at the end of this work assumes the widest possible range of life experience and degree of theological comprehension in its composition.

Introduction

To be or not to be in love?

There is a story told of that great Victorian, Thomas Carlyle. One day he returned from Sunday morning service in a bad temper. He said to his mother, over brunch, "I cannot think why they preach such long sermons. If I were a minister, I would go up into the pulpit and say no more than this: 'Good People, you know what you ought to do. Now go out and do it!'" His mother replied, "Aye, Thomas, but would you not tell them how?"[1]

Do we "good people" know what we ought to do and how to love? Humanity has yet to produce a completely satisfying solution to the question, "To what degree should the heart and head be followed in matters of love?" Many tend to trust the promptings of their hearts as sure guides in determining what is good, true, and beautiful in life. For such people love is, in its essence and by its signs, primarily a feeling. Common convictions that arise out of the immoderate and unreflective extremes of this perspective include the following: Love, whether instilling feelings of enthrallment and elevation, or conveying the experience of falling, is a thrilling concoction of passion and romance. Love is a spontaneous product of good fortune more than conscious choice, and as such it is a sublime reality that lies beyond personal control. Love is thus regarded as always a risky business fraught with prospects of potential hurt and loss on one hand, and a sense of supreme fulfillment and contentment on the other. For those who love "from the heart," love lives as long as the feeling of love lasts, and when the feeling dies, love is no more.

Love is often thought to be no less served by oversight by the head, or intellect, as well as by the promptings from the heart. A marginal form of this conviction is "to love is to know." It is thus thought that a great impediment to love is the lack of knowledge of specific facts about the beloved. A love relationship greatly depends upon the ability to jointly inform or share thoughts, feelings, hopes, and dreams. Being a better lover requires knowing about and commanding various kinds of expertise in the ways of love. One must develop these skills by which relationships are fostered, communication is facilitated, intimacy is experienced, and sex is made ever more satisfying. Love is supposedly mutual, reciprocal, conditional, measurable, and quantifiable.

Dimensions of loving that touch upon emotions and intellect, though they easily lead to superficial conclusions, are not to be facilely dismissed. The role that emotions and intellect play in nurturing a love that is lasting, faithful, and life-giving should in no way be disregarded or undervalued. Yet, for Jesus, loving is not following the heart and head as if "What do I feel?" and "What do I think and know?" are the determinative questions on the subject of love. Rather, the important question is: "To be or not to be in love?" The question is posed quite apart from the notions that love is a feeling or a degree of acquired knowledge about the other who is loved. This is to say, love is a freely imparted and freely chosen state of being. Pope Benedict XVI teaches in his 2006 encyclical, *Deus Caritas Est* (God Is Love, hereafter, *DCE*, with section number), that we can be "commanded" to love because we have first been loved (*DCE* 14). We have been created in and for love. We can willfully choose to accept or reject being in love; this principle "is the starting point for understanding the great parables of Jesus" (*DCE* 15).

Jesus, the Master Lover, is also a master storyteller. Rather than give long sermons Jesus employed short parables that engage the listener emotionally, intellectually, and spiritually. These stories describe for us the nature of true love that is most appropriate in God's kingdom of life and love. The stories instruct us on how to distinguish true love from cheap imitations. Through these stories Jesus teaches us how to act lovingly and invites us to be in love at all times and in every place. The good news about this love is that it is not a "happening" to be wished for and dreamed about: Christian love is real, and we can be in this love this very day, in this very moment.

Here we will follow the recommendation of eminent theologian and preacher Walter Burghardt, SJ, with regard to one of church history's greatest preachers, St. John Chrysostom (Chrysostom, meaning, "golden mouth"), the fifth-century patriarch of Constantinople. Burghardt strongly urged that St. John's "passionate attachment to St. Paul" be noted and imitated, and that it would be a point of deep regret should the "Pauline Christ" go unproclaimed.[2] Jesus' love stories featured in this book are ordered by what is probably the most familiar and frequently quoted scripture passage on the nature of love, St. Paul's First Letter to the Corinthians, chapter 13, verses 4–8:

> Love is patient; love is kind; love is not
> envious or boastful or arrogant or rude. It
> does not insist on its own way; it is not
> irritable or resentful; it does not rejoice
> in wrongdoing, but rejoices in the truth.
> It bears all things, believes all things,
> hopes all things, endures all things. Love
> never ends.

Each chapter will address questions about love that have been commonly put to sages and philosophers, interpersonal relations experts, and advice columnists through the ages, questions such as: How do I know if I am in love or that somebody loves me? Who is the right person for me to love? How long must I wait for love? Who are the greatest lovers on earth? When it comes to love, why am I not as fortunate or happy as others? I have been hurt in love; how do I avoid being hurt again?

Accompanying each of Jesus' stories will be one or more of his prescriptions, precepts, and tenets on love. This section, entitled "The Word of Love," is intended to help the reader reflect on the mystery of Christian love.

Before reading these love stories

No matter how open we feel or think we are to love, we cannot begin to fathom the mystery of true Christian loving without putting aside our preconceptions and cultural biases regarding feelings and knowledge. If we are to be open to the Master Lover's teachings, we must abandon, at least temporarily, our preference for loving "from the heart" or "out of our heads" and make a leap of faith. For the former kind of lovers, the leap of faith is to accept that "love is not a feeling"[3] and to be aware that "love is not merely a sentiment....A sentiment can be a marvelous first spark, but it is not the fullness of love" (DCE 17). Those who attend to the intellect are to accept that love is not a matter of human wisdom or knowledge (1 Cor 1:18–25), and are to be aware that "the love proclaimed by Jesus consists of the very fact that in God and with God we love even the person whom [we] do not like or even know" (*DCE* 18). The "faith-based" love described in these stories requires a profound trust in the power of love. To be in love requires a leap of faith, a conscious act of the will that originates from a place within us that is deeper than our deepest feelings and emotions, and extends to a realm beyond that which the mind can fully grasp.

Jesus' faith-based love is radical exactly because it lies beyond feelings and conventional thinking and requires us to live "outside the box." "The box," in this case, is our minds. (In fact, his own relatives once said of Jesus that he had "gone out of his mind"—Mark 3:21.) Besides storing in our heads the "wheat" of rational and functional ways of thinking, we also keep there the "weeds" of irrational and dysfunctional ways of thinking, cultural biases, personal prejudices, and programming that we have learned. Trying to live off a diet of these weeds, we ought not be surprised at finding ourselves "sick" and "imprisoned," unhappy, bored, and hurting.

For example, many have swallowed the weed that words, mere human words, possess power. As social beings humans need signs and symbols to communicate with others, through language, gestures, rituals, and actions. The same holds true for our relationship with God *within which we all are conceived.*[4] But we have come to believe that words that are detached from the power of this truth possess power in themselves to hurt or heal. Following this line of thinking we expend our energies on controlling what others say and the way they say it. We put ourselves at the mercy of what others might say about or to us. We put hope in the notion that "communication" solves our problems, fixes our relationships, and saves our marriages. We spend our lives sharing our feelings, thoughts, and stories. We strive to become experts in communicating how we feel and what is on our minds. We remake our world into one in which communication is not only instant but constant. Yet, for all of our words, communicating, and sharing, we are not any closer to staying together, finding solutions for our problems, or living fruitful and peaceful lives. We are great communicators of everything but love.

Another issue about which Jesus thinks "outside the box" is relationships. The relationships that we are most familiar with and that receive most of our attention are of the human-made variety. They are relationships we have, work at, and foster. At the same time, however, we speak about these relationships as though they have a mind, will, and life of their own. They can choose to work or not work. They can will themselves to be loving or dysfunctional. They even have the power to mysteriously or magically come into and pass out of existence.

In Jesus' teaching and his love stories the only relationships that exist "outside" our minds are the ones that are divinely created by the Master Lover, are sustained and maintained by him, and last forever. For example, when Jesus makes the statement, "I am the vine, you are the branches" (John 15:5), he is defining the relationship that exists between him and us.

Whether we are connected to Jesus in life and love or disconnected from him, the relationship of vine to branches exists. The vine and not the relationship is always the source of our life and love. Jesus maintains the relationship he has with us branches so that we might pass on his sacrificial love to those who are in need of the life-giving "fruit," deeds, and works of love. This divinely created, sustained, and everlasting relationship is, as Pope John Paul II describes, "a dynamic relationship of faithful self-giving with others. It is in the faithful self-giving [and not in the relationship] that a person finds a fullness of certainty and security."[5] Hence, the gift of life and love that we receive from the vine we give as a gift of our lives and ourselves to others with whom we are already in relationships that the Master Lover has created. (See Story 4: "The Good Neighbor.")

The difference between a human-made relationship that Dave Barry (syndicated columnist, author, and Pulitzer prize winner) says is a "nebulous and imprecise concept" or an idea that is planted in the brain "by constantly making subtle references to it in…everyday conversations"[6] and Jesus' divinely created outside-the-brain relationship can be seen in the love story of "The Loving Father and His Two Insensitive Sons" (Story 6). Because the two sons are fixated on their own happiness, they do what many of us have done. They give up on "love" and replace it with "relationship." Both sons use the relationship they have with their father in an attempt to extort from him what they think they must have in order to be happy. Human relationships ultimately are about ourselves primarily and only secondarily about the other. The father, on the other hand, sees the divinely created relationship he is in with his sons as the reason he will always love them no matter what they say to him or how they try to hurt him. That "he will always be their father" does not mean he will always have authority over them, but that he will always love them by accepting them, welcoming them into his home, and giving them whatever food, clothing, and shelter they need. Because the sons' brains are awash with ideas about relationships and what will make them happy, they are "lost" and "dead" to the love their father has for them.

Before reading this book, we must be prepared to think "outside the box" with regard to love stories in general. Having grown up on a steady diet of romantic fairy tales of princes and princesses, we are accustom to having our love stories end with a couple "living happily ever after." Even if one should die tragically, that is, "young" and "before one's time," we attempt to find some happiness in thinking that we can keep them alive (as if we had the power to keep them alive) in our heads by remembering them or in our hearts by feeling something for them. Such love stories are not about being in love but about being happy. The weed of doing things in order to be happy has taken over our minds to the extent that we have twisted the right to pursue happiness into a right to be happy. We attach our happiness to having a relationship, to marrying whomever we desire, to acquiring whatever we want, and to behaving however we feel. If we should ever be unhappy, it is never our fault. It is always someone else or society that is the cause of our unhappiness and bears the responsibility for making us happy. In this kind of love story, we are the center of the universe and the story is all about us and our happiness.

A popular proverb, commonly attributed to Confucius and to rabbis says, If you want to be happy for an hour, take a nap. If you want to be happy for a day, attend a sumptuous banquet. If you want to be happy for a week, go fishing. If you want to be happy for a month, get married. However, if you want to be happy the rest of your life, spend your whole life serving others.

Jesus' love stories are not about being happy. They are about being in love. To be in love we must live outside the "box" of what will make us happy. To be in love we must lay our lives down for others. The love in which we spend our lives in serving others will not give us the temporary happiness of romantic love stories but, rather, the lasting, everyday, all-one's-life-and-then-some happiness Jesus refers to as *joy*. Jesus tells us his stories of love and commands us to love by giving ourselves away to others so that his joy, his eternal happiness, might be in us and our joy might be complete (John 15:9–17).

To reiterate: Jesus was not afraid to get out of the cultural thought process and the conventional "wisdom" of his day. He is to be followed by us in our day. The Master Lover was not afraid to go beyond reflexively accepted thoughts and feelings to live "outside the box." In deed and in word, Jesus gets out of his mind to live the reality of love. Unless we are willing to set our own received notions aside and be open to the "wheat" of Jesus' love that heals, nourishes, and frees us, there is much about which we are "lost" and to which we are "dead."

Looking at our world and each other through the narrow prism of our feelings, thinking hinders the ability to make sense of what Jesus has to say and show us about love. One cannot import a file onto the hard drive of a computer already containing a file with the same title until the existing file is renamed. Because we already have a file on love in our heads, we find it difficult to comprehend what Jesus is telling us through his love stories. In order to give Jesus' file or program of love an impartial and unbiased hearing, we must rename, at least temporarily, our version of love to be something other than love. This is a daunting undertaking, and there are many of us who are too afraid to take that risk. Our fear is not so much a fear of the new and unknown in Jesus' way of love; it is the fear of leaving behind the place we have and familiar ways of feeling and thinking. For those of us who hesitate to make this bold and adventurous step, we can take some solace in this: If, after examining and trying Jesus' way of love, we do not experience more peace and greater freedom, we can delete Jesus' version of love and go back to our old ways of loving. If, on the other hand, we do find greater peace, freedom, healing, and happiness in Jesus' love, we can relegate what we thought love was to the recycle bin in favor of the Master's way of being in love. If, after an unprejudiced reading of *Jesus' Love Stories,* one wishes to reject love rooted in faith for a love based on feelings and knowledge, that, too, is a subject for one's choice. Whatever way of love one chooses, the option is deeply personal and entirely one's own. May we remember, though, that when our feelings change or deceive us, and all our knowledge about love leaves us unfulfilled, being in Jesus' love forever and acting only out of love that never ends is the way that is always open.

STORY 1
The Bridegroom and the Impatient Bridesmaids

How long should I wait for somebody to love me?

*T*hen the kingdom of heaven will be like this. Ten bridesmaids took their lamps and went to meet the bridegroom. Five of them were foolish, and five were wise. When the foolish took their lamps, they took no oil with them; but the wise took flasks of oil with their lamps. As the bridegroom was delayed, all of them became drowsy and slept. But at midnight there was a shout, "Look! Here is the bridegroom! Come out to meet him." Then all those bridesmaids got up and trimmed their lamps.

The foolish said to the wise, "Give us some of your oil, for our lamps are going out." But the wise replied, "No! there will not be enough for you and for us; you had better go to the dealers and buy some for yourselves." And while they went to buy it, the bridegroom came, and those who were ready went with him into the wedding banquet; and the door was shut. Later the other bridesmaids came also, saying, "Lord, lord, open to us." But he replied, "Truly I tell you, I do not know you." Keep awake therefore, for you know neither the day nor the hour. (Matt 25:1–13)

These two groups of bridesmaids represent two different and distinct approaches to love. The bridesmaids whose lamps go out for lack of oil are foolish. They believe that love is a *feeling*. Impatient, they believe that they lack the passion necessary to wait and watch for the bridegroom. They go in search of emotional oil to fuel the flames of their love. In listening to their feelings they miss their opportunity to be in love. When the bridegroom, love, does come for them, they are off chasing a feeling. Although the foolish think that love has shut them out, it is actually they who have closed the door on their experience of being loved. Their belief that love is a feeling keeps them from joining in the wedding feast and from being in love.

As St. Paul says, "love is patient" (1 Cor 13:4). The bridesmaids who have enough oil to keep their lamps burning brightly are wise. They can patiently wait for love because their faith in love includes the unshakable belief that they are loved and, therefore, are lovable. Like their foolish sisters, the wise bridesmaids experience the whole range of human emotions. They feel everything from impatience and being unloved to the feelings of patience and being loved. Unlike the foolish, the wise do not mistakenly identify themselves with their feelings. If, for instance, they should feel impatient they do not think themselves to *be* impatient. They believe that they have a reservoir of patience and love within them. They have enough of the oil of patience and love to get them through the longest and coldest nights. This kind of patience "comes from knowing one is loved by God, chosen to live forever with the Holy Trinity."[1]

To the foolish this makes no sense. Because they identify so completely with their thoughts and feelings, not acting in accord with them seems hypocritical. The bridegroom does not recognize the foolish bridesmaids because they do not know themselves who they are. To the wise, acting patiently and lovingly despite what they feel or think makes perfect sense. The wise bridesmaids know themselves to *be* patient and loved and, thus, are ready to enter the wedding feast when the bridegroom, love, arrives.

The Word of Love
Love is patient. (1 Cor 13:4)

For thus said the Lord God, the Holy
One of Israel: In returning and rest you
shall be saved; in quietness and in trust
shall be your strength. (Isa 30:15)

The Discerning Shepherd and the Unkind Goats

Who are the lovers on earth?

When the Son of Man comes in his glory, and all the angels with him, then he will sit on the throne of his glory. All the nations will be gathered before him, and he will separate people one from another as a shepherd separates the sheep from the goats, and he will put the sheep at his right hand and the goats at the left. Then the king will say to those at his right hand, "Come, you that are blessed by my Father, inherit the kingdom prepared for you from the foundation of the world; for I was hungry and you gave me food, I was *thirsty and you gave me something to drink, I was a stranger and you welcomed me, I was naked and you gave me clothing, I was sick and you took care of me, I was in prison and you visited me." Then the righteous will answer him, "Lord, when was it that we saw you hungry and gave you food, or thirsty and gave you something to drink? And when was it that we saw you a stranger and welcomed you, or naked and gave you clothing? And when was it that we saw you sick or in prison and visited you?" And the king will answer them, "Truly I tell you, just as you did it to one of the least of these who are members of my family, you did it to me." Then he will say to those at his left hand, "You that are accursed, depart from me into the eternal fire prepared for the devil and his angels; for I was hungry and you gave me no food, I was thirsty and you gave me nothing to drink, I was a stranger and you did not welcome me, naked and you did not give me clothing, sick and in prison and you did not visit me." Then they also will answer, "Lord, when was it that we saw you hungry or thirsty or a stranger or naked or sick or in prison, and did not take care of you?" Then he will answer them, "Truly I tell you, just as you did not do it to one of the least of these, you did not do it to me." And these will go away into eternal punishment, but the righteous into eternal life. (Matt 25:31–46)*

According to this story the Master Lover will not judge the peoples of the world at the end of time after the manner of a courtroom judge. He will not weigh the evidence of our good and bad deeds and render a verdict one way or another. He will not even judge us as deserving of reward or punishment. Rather, the Master Lover will be like a shepherd who can see the difference between a sheep and a goat and separates them accordingly. "The criterion for the definitive decision about a human life's worth or lack thereof" is love (*DCE* 15). The Master Lover will simply look at us and separate "the sheep," those of us who are in *love*, from "the goats," those of us who are not. Being welcomed into the kingdom is not so much a matter of judgment on God's part as it is the consequence of the choosing on our part to be or not to be in love.

Love is kind. The sheep the Master Lover places on his right are the greatest lovers on earth because they are kind to everyone they meet. "This love does not simply offer people material help but refreshment and care for their souls" (*DCE* 28). If they see someone, anyone, who is hungry, naked, or homeless, they share their resources of food, clothing, and shelter with that person. If they see someone who is sick or imprisoned, they help that person. If the person they visit is sick of heart they offer the "medicine" of "the look of love they crave" (*DCE* 18). To the person who is prisoner of his/her fears, feelings, and irrational thinking, they offer the keys of the truth of love that can be used to unlock one's mind and set oneself free.

What distinguishes these true master lovers from those who feel and think they are is that the former kind of loving is nonjudgmental. The goats that the Master Lover consigns to his left are already in a bad place. They are already in hell but do not know it. They have chosen not to be in love by acting kindly to *some* but not to *all* they meet. Selective kindness, loving, and caring are *not* love. If kindness is not inclusive, it is not love. The goats are not in love because they discriminated between those toward whom they were kind and those toward whom they were not. They chose the recipients of their love based on how they felt toward them at the moment, what they thought about them, and how important their relationship with them was. Not to love everyone we meet is not to love anyone we meet or know. Do the quantity and quality of our acts of love matter if we do not have love? Without being in love we do nothing and are nothing (cf. 1 Cor 13:1–3). The consequence of choosing such judgmental behavior is ending up in the state of not being in love, which is also known as hell.

The greatest lovers on earth are simply and completely in love. Being kind to anyone they meet is such a part of who they are that they do not feel or think they are special. They are kind to all without any thought of reward or punishment. It has been said that these lovers do not spend five seconds a year wondering whether they are going to heaven or hell. Why? They are busy focusing not on themselves and what they are feeling, but on meeting the real needs of the hungry, naked, homeless, sick, and imprisoned. The righteousness of their love does not come from having the proper feelings or thoughts but from doing what is right at the right time, in the right place, and for the right reasons. The consequence of choosing to live with such love is eternal life.

The Word of Love
Love is kind. (1 Cor 13:4)

> If I speak in the tongues of mortals and of angels, but do not have love, I am a noisy gong or a clanging cymbal. And if I have prophetic powers, and understand all mysteries and all knowledge, and if I have all faith, so as to remove mountains, but do not have love, I am nothing. If I give away all my possessions, and if I hand over my body so that I may boast, but do not have love, I gain nothing.
>
> (1 Cor 13:1–3)

> Do not judge, and you will not be judged; do not condemn, and you will not be condemned. Forgive, and you will be forgiven; give, and it will be given to

you. A good measure, pressed down, shaken together, running over, will be put into your lap; for the measure you give will be the measure you get back.
(Luke 6:37–38)

The Generous Vintner and the Envious Day Laborers

When it comes to love, why am I not as fortunate or happy as others?

*F*or the kingdom of heaven is like a landowner who went out early in the morning to hire laborers for his vineyard. After agreeing with the laborers for the usual daily wage, he sent them into his vineyard. When he went out about nine o'clock, he saw others standing idle in the market-place; and he said to them, "You also go into the vine-yard, and I will pay you whatever is right." So they went. When he went out again about noon and about three o'clock, he did the same. And about five o'clock *he went out and found others standing around; and he said to them, "Why are you standing here idle all day?" They said to him, "Because no one has hired us." He said to them, "You also go into the vineyard." When evening came, the owner of the vineyard said to his manager, "Call the laborers and give them their pay, beginning with the last and then going to the first." When those hired about five o'clock came, each of them received the usual daily wage. Now when the first came, they thought they would receive more; but each of them also received the usual daily wage. And when they received it, they grumbled against the landowner, saying, "These last worked only one hour, and you have made them equal to us who have borne the burden of the day and the scorching heat." But he replied to one of them, "Friend, I am doing you no wrong; did you not agree with me for the usual daily wage? Take what belongs to you and go; I choose to give to this last the same as I give to you. Am I not allowed to do what I choose with what belongs to me? Or are you envious because I am generous?" So the last will be first, and the first will be last. (Matt 20:1–16)*

Love is the service we carry out to attend constantly to human suffering and an individual's needs, including material needs (*DCE* 19). Because the generous landowner loves his employees, he is free to do what he pleases with his money. What pleases him is to put the things he has power over at the service of his employees. He loves those who work the entire day by paying them a fair wage, one on which they can live. To those who through no fault of their own did not find enough work, he gives money to feed their families. This landowner puts his employees' welfare and well-being ahead of his own self-interests and personal gain.

St. Basil the Great asserted that "we possess from the first moment of our existence an innate power and ability to love."[1] Will we employ this power to use things and love people for their benefit, or to love things and use people for our personal gain? The way the landowner used his money to feed people demonstrates his love for his fellow human beings. The disgruntled day laborers, on the other hand, are envious of the landowner's money and their fellow laborers good fortune of being given enough to feed their families that day.

In an economy based on day labor, as in all economies, inequalities exist. The day a worker does not work is the day his family goes hungry. "It is true that the pursuit of justice must be a fundamental norm of the State and that the aim of a just social order is to guarantee to each person, according to the principle of subsidiarity, his share of the community's goods" (*DCE* 26). However, "love—*caritas*—will always prove necessary even in the most just society. There is no ordering of the state so just that it can eliminate the need for a service of love" (*DCE* 28). The generous vintner is happy that he has the wherewithal to provide this service of love to those who are in need of daily bread. Because of their envy, the grumbling day laborers succeed only in turning their morning joy of finding work for a fair and agreed upon wage into an evening of discontent, resentment, and unhappiness.

Like the envious day laborers, we will feel cheated and think some injustice has occurred when we compare what others have to what we do not have. When we desire the wealth and happiness that others seem to have, our envy causes us to live sad lives of quiet desperation and loneliness. Rather, by putting the interests and well-being of others before our own self-interests and feelings, we open ourselves to the experience of love. Being grateful over the good fortune of our neighbors and generously putting our resources at the service of those in need opens us to the good fortune, the happiness, and the joy of being in love.

The Word of Love
Love is not envious....(1 Cor 13:4)

> For the love of money is a root of all kinds of evil, and in their eagerness to be rich some have wandered away from the faith and pierced themselves with many pains. (1 Tim 6:10)

> No one can serve two masters; for a slave will either hate the one and love the other, or be devoted to the one and

despise the other. You cannot serve God and wealth. (Matt 6:24)

Like good stewards of the manifold grace of God, serve one another with whatever gift each of you has received. (1 Pet 4:10)

The Good Neighbor

Who is the right person for me to love?

*J*ust then a lawyer stood up to test Jesus. "Teacher," he said, "what must I do to inherit eternal life?" He said to him, "What is written in the law? What do you read there?" He answered, "You shall love the Lord your God with all your heart, and with all your soul, and with all your strength, and with all your mind; and your neighbor as yourself." And he said to him, "You have given the right answer; do this, and you will live." But wanting to justify himself, he asked Jesus, "And who is my neighbor?" Jesus replied, "A man was *going down from Jerusalem to Jericho, and fell into the hands of robbers, who stripped him, beat him, and went away, leaving him half dead. Now by chance a priest was going down that road; and when he saw him, he passed by on the other side. So likewise a Levite, when he came to the place and saw him, passed by on the other side. But a Samaritan while traveling came near him; and when he saw him, he was moved with pity. He went to him and bandaged his wounds, having poured oil and wine on them. Then he put him on his own animal, brought him to an inn, and took care of him. The next day he took out two denarii, gave them to the innkeeper, and said, 'Take care of him; and when I come back, I will repay you whatever more you spend.' Which of these three, do you think, was a neighbor to the man who fell into the hands of the robbers?" He said, "The one who showed him mercy." Jesus said to him, "Go and do likewise." (Luke 10:25–37)*

"Until that time [of Jesus], the concept of neighbor was understood as referring essentially to one's countrymen and to foreigners who had settled in the land of Israel; in other words, to the closely knit community of a single country or people" (*DCE* 15). Jesus' parable of the Good Samaritan abolishes that limit and requires that love be shown to the needy we encounter "by chance" whoever they may be (*DCE* 25).

At the time of the telling of this love story the animosity between Jews and Samaritans was visceral. As closely situated neighbors and long-estranged kin, Jews and Samaritans were not strangers to each other. They knew and despised one another. What makes this parable a premier story of love is its assertion that love is possible even if one has been raised with deep-seated prejudices and feelings against others.

The Jews in this story pass by one of their own who lies injured alongside the road. They could assuage their conscience for not attending to the half-dead man by thinking that they could "boast" that they had kept a religious regulation. They make the judgment that this was not the right time, the right set of circumstances, or the right person to love.

The Samaritan, in spite of feelings and thoughts to the contrary, goes out of his way to provide lifesaving assistance to the unfortunate Jew who was left by robbers and his co-religionists to die. The Samaritan even goes "the extra mile" by providing for the victim's long-term care and recovery.

Love is not a matter of boasting that we have "fallen in love" or have found the right person to love. We are pompous and full of ourselves when we choose to love one person but not another on the basis of our feelings and thoughts. "Following the example given in the parable of the good Samaritan, Christian charity is first of all the simple response to immediate needs and specific situations: feeding the hungry, clothing the naked, caring for and healing the sick, visiting those in prison, etc." (*DCE* 31). We love rightly when we do not allow our personal feelings or what we think about someone to keep us from acting mercifully by taking whatever course of action that allows the person to live. The right person for us to love is our neighbor, especially one who is in need. No particular feelings are required to love another, nor should we allow any feelings to prevent us from providing needed assistance. Because there is no one who is undeserving of our love, we cannot make a mistake in loving our neighbor. There are no wrong people that we cannot love. We are in love and we love the right person when we are the good Samaritans who act compassionately and kindly toward anyone we meet along the road we are traveling.

The Word of Love
Love is not boastful....(1 Cor 13:4)

> Then he said to them, "Is it lawful to do good or to do harm on the sabbath, to save life or to kill?" (Mark 3:4)

> But I say to you that listen, Love your enemies, do good to those who hate you, bless those who curse you, pray for those who abuse you....Do to others as you would have them do to you. If you love those who love you, what credit is that

to you? For even sinners love those who love them. If you do good to those who do good to you, what credit is that to you? For even sinners do the same. (Luke 6:27–28, 31–33)

STORY 5
The Arrogant Pharisee and the Humble Tax-Collector

How do I know if I love someone?

e also told this parable to some who trusted in themselves that they were righteous and regarded others with contempt: "Two men went up to the temple to pray, one a Pharisee and the other a tax-collector. The Pharisee, standing by himself, was praying thus, 'God, I thank you that I am not like other people: thieves, rogues, adulterers, or even like this tax-collector. I fast twice a week; I give a tenth of all my income.' But the tax-collector, standing far off, would not even look up to heaven, but was beating his breast and saying, 'God, be merciful to me, a sinner!' I tell you, this man went down to his home justified rather than the other; for all who exalt themselves will be humbled, but all who humble themselves will be exalted." (Luke 18:9–14)

The Pharisee "never discerned in the Scriptures the love story of God and the world he created and so loved that he would give his only-begotten Son that it might be saved."[1] He thinks that his relationship with God is a matter of juridical weighing of legal prescriptions and the vindication of rights. The Pharisee arrogantly measures his love against the love with which others love, such as that of the tax-collector. He vainly thinks and feels that his love is better, deeper, truer, and more real than the tax-collector's.

For the arrogant, love is the vanity of all vanities. Vain lovers are all too ready to count the ways they love someone in a conceited effort to prove to themselves and everyone around them that they love more deeply and truly than they are loved. They measure their love by feelings, emotions, and physical gratification. They keep careful track of all they do for the object of their love, the things they give, and the times they think of them. Since they are self-righteous, no one can possibly love them as much as they love. They are right about everything: what is and is not love, what the signs of love are, the kind and depth of feelings the other should have, and what the other should be doing for the sake of their relationship.

At the very moment of any perceived indifference, betrayal, or failure to live up to the demands of the relationship, the feelings of vain lovers turn suddenly and violently into those of hurt, hatred, or anger, or into that of simple indifference.[2]

The proper way of loving others leads to humility, not arrogance. The ones who truly love do not consider themselves superior to the ones who are loved (*DCE* 35). Because the tax-collector is honest about what love is and who he is, he acknowledges something that the Pharisee in his arrogance and conceit can never admit. The tax-collector does not know if he in fact is loving or not. Since he cannot trust his feelings or thoughts to tell him, the tax-collector can only trust that he is in love. Unlike the Pharisee, the tax-collector makes no attempt to count the ways that he loves or to justify himself before God. Instead, he humbly asks the Master Lover for mercy and forgiveness for the times he failed to love. Having received God's blessing, the tax-collector returns home to love his family with the same love.

The Word of Love
Love is not...arrogant.... (1 Cor 13:4)

> Do nothing from selfish ambition or conceit, but in humility regard others as better than yourselves. Let each of you look not to your own interests, but to the interests of others. (Phil 2:3–4)

All who exalt themselves will be humbled, and all who humble themselves will be exalted. (Matt 23:12)

So you also, when you have done all that you were ordered to do, say, "We are worthless slaves; we have done only what we ought to have done!" (Luke 17:10)

STORY 6
The Loving Father and His Two Insensitive Sons

How do I know if somebody loves me?

*T*hen Jesus said, "There was a man who had two sons. The younger of them said to his father, 'Father, give me the share of the property that will belong to me.' So he divided his property between them. A few days later the younger son gathered all he had and traveled to a distant country, and there he squandered his property in dissolute living. When he had spent everything, a severe famine took place throughout that country, and he began to be in need. So he went and hired himself out to one of the citizens of that coun-

try, who sent him to his fields to feed the pigs. He would gladly have filled himself with the pods that the pigs were eating; and no one gave him anything. But when he came to himself he said, 'How many of my father's hired hands have bread enough and to spare, but here I am dying of hunger! I will get up and go to my father, and I will say to him, "Father, I have sinned against heaven and before you; I am no longer worthy to be called your son; treat me like one of your hired hands."' So he set off and went to his father. But while he was still far off, his father saw him and was filled with compassion; he ran and put his arms around him and kissed him. Then the son said to him, 'Father, I have sinned against heaven and before you; I am no longer worthy to be called your son.' But the father said to his slaves, 'Quickly, bring out a robe—the best one—and put it on him; put a ring on his finger and sandals on his feet. And get the fatted calf and kill it, and let us eat and celebrate; for this son of mine was dead and is alive again; he was lost and is found!' And they began to celebrate. Now his elder son was in the field; and when he came and approached the house, he heard music and dancing. He called one of the slaves and asked what was going on. He replied, 'Your brother has come, and your father has killed the fatted calf, because he has got him back safe and sound.' Then he became angry and refused to go in. His father came out and began to plead with him. But he answered his father, 'Listen! For all these years I have been working like a slave for you, and I have never disobeyed your command; yet you have never given me even a young goat so that I might celebrate with my friends. But when this son of yours came back, who has devoured your property with prostitutes, you killed the fatted calf for him!' Then the father said to him, 'Son, you are always with me, and all that is mine is yours. But we had to celebrate and rejoice, because this brother of yours was dead and has come to life; he was lost and has been found.'" (Luke 15:11–32)

The two sons in this story are completely unaware of how much their father loves them. They do not experience their father's love because they are insensitive. They do not recognize love when they see it because they are insensitive to what their father thinks and how he feels. They are self-absorbed. They think only of themselves, how they feel, and what they want. This insensitivity to others manifests itself in the rude way the sons treat their father. In attempts to get what they desire, they both devise plans to get what they want.

The younger son callously tells his father that he is worth more to him dead than alive. He demands an inheritance before his father is dead so that with his father's money he can live a life to which he feels he is entitled. No amount of talking, reasoning, or saying "I love you. Don't go" on his father's part can break through the boy's insensitivity. Even the offer of giving him half of the inheritance before he dies as a sign that he loves him as much as his older brother does not have any effect on him. The younger son is senseless, "dead." Not until he experiences the lack of love for him in the world does he wake up and "come to his senses." He realizes how much his father loves him and what a blind fool he was not to see this. He realizes that his father loves his hired hands because he saw to it that they always had more than enough to eat. He realizes that his father always loved him and showed his love by feeding, clothing, and sheltering him. The prodigal son returns home humble and contrite to the father who expresses his love for his hungry, naked, homeless son by giving him a welcoming embrace, feeding him a feast, clothing him with robe, ring, and sandals, and sheltering him in his own home.

Envious of his brother, the older son devises his own plan to get what he wants. He thinks that if he could just make his father feel guilty he could shame him into giving him whatever he desires. The older son rudely blames his father for his own unhappiness. He then, with indignant insensitivity, accuses the father of being insensitive to his feelings and needs! The father cannot make his son see how much he loves him. The father can only respond to his son's complaints by pointing out to him that everything he has in the way of food, clothing, and shelter has always been unconditionally available to the son.

"Love is not…rude" (1 Cor 13:5). What is rude is blaming others for our unhappiness. We are insensitive when we think that our happiness depends upon what others do or do not do, say or do not say, to us. As long as we focus on what we think and how we feel, we will remain insensitive, that is, "dead," to the love others have for us. When we stop obsessing on getting what we think and feel will make us happy and stop blaming others for our past and present unhappiness, our eyes will be opened to seeing who it is that loves us and who does not.

Love "is first of all the simple response to immediate needs and specific situations: feeding the hungry, clothing the naked, caring for and healing the sick, visiting those in prison, etc." (*DCE* 31). When we come to our senses, we will recognize that we are loved and who it is that loves us.

The Word of Love
Love is not…rude. (1 Cor 13:5)

> Those who say, "I love God," and hate their brothers or sisters, are liars; for those who do not love a brother or sister whom they have seen, cannot love God whom they have not seen. (1 John 4:20)

The Charitable Landowner and the Jealous Tenants

Is jealousy a sign of love?

*L*isten to another parable. There was a landowner who planted a vineyard, put a fence around it, dug a wine press in it, and built a watch-tower. Then he leased it to tenants and went to another country. When the harvest time had come, he sent his slaves to the tenants to collect his produce. But the tenants seized his slaves and beat one, killed another, and stoned another. Again he sent other slaves, more than the first; and they treated them in the same way. Finally he sent his son to them, saying, "They will respect my son." But

when the tenants saw the son, they said to them-
selves, "This is the heir; come, let us kill him and get
his inheritance." So they seized him, threw him out
of the vineyard, and killed him. Now when the
owner of the vineyard comes, what will he do to
those tenants? They said to him, "He will put those
wretches to a miserable death, and lease the vine-
yard to other tenants who will give him the produce
at the harvest time." Jesus said to them, "Have you
never read in the scriptures: 'The stone that the
builders rejected has become the cornerstone; this
was the Lord's doing, and it is amazing in our eyes'?
Therefore I tell you, the kingdom of God will be
taken away from you and given to a people that pro-
duces the fruits of the kingdom. The one who falls
on this stone will be broken to pieces; and it will
crush anyone on whom it falls." (Matt 21:33–44)

The ungrateful tenants are jealous of the generous landowner and his son who would inherit the vineyard. They will stop at nothing in order to possess
whatever they have set their hearts and minds on.

It is often said that love is blind. The truth is that
it is not love that is blind; it is jealousy that is blind.
Jealousy blinds the tenants and keeps them from seeing
the evil in abusing, beating, and killing anyone who
stands in the way of getting what they think and feel will

make them happy. Jealousy blinds the tenants to the dignity and worth of every human being. The tenants do not see a person as a human being who has a right to life. In the pursuit of happiness in their own way, they bestow upon themselves whatever "rights" they require to obtain what they desire.

Jealous lovers treat the subject of their affection not as a person but as a "thing," object, trophy, or prize. The jealous try to convince themselves that they care for the other. The recipients of such jealousy may at first also think that the attention they are getting and the deep feelings the jealous lover has for them are signs of how much they are loved. Neither the jealous lover nor the jealously loved realize that such "caring" is a sign of obsession. Should the jealously loved awaken to the situation they are in, the feelings of being loved and cared about are quickly replaced with the awful sense of being held captive, suffocated, or emotionally choked to death. Because the jealous do not see the evil in the violent means they employ to obtain and possess the object of their obsession, they have no boundaries. They do not hesitate to destroy anyone, even the ones they say they love and care about, rather than lose what they think and feel rightfully belongs to them.

As happened to the wretched tenants in the story, jealous lovers also come to a bad end. Their jealousy is the cause of their downfall. Insisting on having everything their own way, they lose everything. Blindly attempting to save their lives by taking the lives of others, they lose their lives (Mark 8:35). The Master Lover sees to it that this story has a happy ending. Those who give themselves rights lose the vineyard. Those who produce and bring forth a bounty by losing their lives in faithful service to others gain the vineyard. "It is in this faithful self-giving that a person finds a fullness of certainty and security."[1]

The Word of Love
Love....does not insist on its own way. (1 Cor 13:5)

But if you have bitter envy and selfish ambition in your hearts, do not be boastful and false to the truth. Such wisdom does not come down from above, but is earthly, unspiritual, devilish. For where there is envy and selfish ambition, there will also be disorder and wickedness of every kind. But the wisdom from above is first pure, then peaceable, gentle, willing to yield, full of mercy and good fruits, without a trace of partiality or hypocrisy. (Jas 3:14–17)

You shall not covet your neighbor's house; you shall not covet your neighbor's wife...or anything that belongs to your neighbor. (Exod 20:17)

STORY 8
The Forgiving King and the Angry Steward

How can I experience love?

*F*or this reason the kingdom of heaven may be compared to a king who wished to settle accounts with his slaves. When he began the reckoning, one who owed him ten thousand talents was brought to him; and, as he could not pay, his lord ordered him to be sold, together with his wife and children and all his possessions, and payment to be made. So the slave fell on his knees before him, saying, "Have patience with me, and I will pay you everything." And out of pity for him, the lord of that slave released him and forgave him the debt. But *that same slave, as he went out, came upon one of his fellow-slaves who owed him a hundred denarii; and seizing him by the throat, he said, "Pay what you owe." Then his fellow-slave fell down and pleaded with him, "Have patience with me, and I will pay you." But he refused; then he went and threw him into prison until he should pay the debt. When his fellow-slaves saw what had happened, they were greatly distressed, and they went and reported to their lord all that had taken place. Then his lord summoned him and said to him, "You wicked slave! I forgave you all that debt because you pleaded with me. Should you not have had mercy on your fellow-slave, as I had mercy on you?" And in anger his lord handed him over to be tortured until he should pay his entire debt. So my heavenly Father will also do to every one of you, if you do not forgive your brother or sister from your heart. (Matt 18:23–35)*

The steward owes the king a huge amount of money. In begging the king to be patient with him, the steward is actually asking him to love him. Instead of loving the steward by being patient with him, the king chooses to love him by forgiving him the entire debt. The experience of being loved is lost by the steward. Although he says he wants to be loved, he wants something else more. When the irritable steward encounters a fellow servant who owes him an insignificant amount, he quickly becomes angry. The quick-tempered steward seizes the servant and starts choking him. He refuses to grant the debtor the love he himself asked of the king. He will not love his fellow servant by being patient with him. He will not love his fellow servant by forgiving the debt that was the smallest fraction of what he owed the king. The loveless, unforgiving steward wants every penny he is owed and, in anger, throws the servant into prison.

Some people would rather be right than happy.[1] The steward would rather receive everything he thinks and feels is rightfully owed him than have the experience of being loved. The steward fails to experience the king's love for him because he refuses to forgive the debt that is owed him. Forgiveness is an act of love by which we act toward those who are indebted to us as if they do not owe us a thing. No matter what the "you-owe-me" is, only after we have forgiven the debt, "let it go," written it off, torn it up, or put it behind us will we have any chance to experience the happiness and joy of being in love.

Being impatient and unforgiving, what the angry steward does experience is a prison of his own making. The experience of not forgiving is one of being locked up and tortured until one finds in oneself the capacity to forgive. For as long as we think that forgiving is a feeling and that having everything that rightfully belongs to us will make us happy, we will languish in our self-made mental prisons. We will suffer terribly and for years if we think that love, patience, forgiveness, and "getting over it" are feelings. As we foolishly wait for a feeling of forgiveness to release us, we will feel, as did the angry steward, that we are the victims of injustice, unfairness, and a violation of our rights. Until we find within ourselves the love to forgive the debts owed to us, we will not experience the joy and freedom of being loved and being in love.

The good news of this love story is that it is within our power to free ourselves from our mental and emotional prisons. The key to experiencing love, both being loved and being in love, is the forgiving king's love for us. There is nothing we cannot forgive our fellow servants because the Master Lover first loved us and has already forgiven us so much more than anyone could ever owe us.[2]

The Word of Love
Love...is not irritable.... (1 Cor 13:5)

> We love because he first loved us. (1 John 4:19)

> And forgive us our sins, for we ourselves forgive everyone indebted to us. (Luke 11:4)

The Innocent Farmer

Does time heal all wounds?

H*e put before them another parable: "The kingdom of heaven may be compared to someone who sowed good seed in his field; but while everybody was asleep, an enemy came and sowed weeds among the wheat, and then went away. So when the plants came up and bore grain, then the weeds appeared as well. And the slaves of the householder came and said to him, 'Master, did you not sow good seed in your field? Where, then, did these weeds come from?' He answered, 'An enemy has done this.' The slaves* *said to him, 'Then do you want us to go and gather them?' But he replied, 'No; for in gathering the weeds you would uproot the wheat along with them. Let both of them grow together until the harvest; and at harvest time I will tell the reapers, Collect the weeds first and bind them in bundles to be burned, but gather the wheat into my barn.'"* (Matt 13:24–30)

Love's power to protect and heal us is far greater than anybody's power to hurt or harm us. The innocent farmer uses the power of love to remain patient and peaceful throughout the crisis he faces. Unlike his frantic and anxious servants, the farmer neither attaches his well-being to that of his fields nor identifies himself with his property. Having removed all emotional investment to the hired hands and his farm, he can see clearly and therefore care appropriately for the others' sake.[1] Protected by the power of love, the farmer does not suffer personally or emotionally from anything his enemy has done to the fields. The innocent farmer does not take offense at his servants' suggestion that he was responsible for the weeds. He is not resentful over what an enemy has done. He is not driven by some compulsion to fix his fields in the vain hope that if external things are restored to perfection he will feel better internally. Instead, the farmer calmly waits until he can clearly discern the weeds from the wheat. Only then does he heal and restore his field by first gathering up the weeds and burning them. Then he harvests the wheat and stores it in his barn.

"Love [does not] brood over injuries."[2] Brooding over our injuries only increases and prolongs our feelings of hurt, guilt, and shame even if we know that we are completely innocent of any wrongdoing. Time does nothing to rid us of our weeds of resentment. If left unchecked, weeds in time take over and destroy the good that flourished in us. Time does not heal anything. Time ages. After years of suffering and brooding over our injuries, all we will have to show for relying on time to heal us is a crop of old wounds and emotional scars that still to this day hurt us when we think of them. Like the weeds in any garden, if we never touch them and allow them to grow they will deeply embed themselves in us. In time, they will take over and ruin us.

Only love has the power to protect and heal. With the power of love we can patiently and peacefully weed the fields and gardens of our minds of the irrational thinking and attachments that are at the root of much of our needless suffering. Following the example of the innocent farmer, we cultivate the wheat of charity and kindness at all times and in every season. Having removed the weeds of our emotional attachment to our feelings and opinions, we experience a healing of all our wounds as the weeds of resentment are burned up in the cauterizing fire of the charity we give to all those we meet, including our enemies.

The Word of Love
Love is not...resentful. (1 Cor 13:5)

Blessed are you when people hate you, and when they exclude you, revile you, and defame you on account of the Son of Man. Rejoice on that day and leap for joy, for surely your reward is great in heaven; for that is what their ancestors did to the prophets. (Luke 6:22–23)

Is it not to share your bread with the hungry, and bring the homeless poor into your house; when you see the naked, to cover them, and not to hide yourself from your own kin? Then your light shall break forth like the dawn, and your healing shall spring up quickly; your vindicator shall go before you, the glory of the Lord shall be your rear guard. (Isa 58:7–8)

The Patient Gardener and the Barren Fig Tree

Why do I exist?

*T*hen he told this parable: "A man had a fig tree planted in his vineyard; and he came looking for fruit on it and found none. So he said to the gardener, 'See here! For three years I have come looking for fruit on this fig tree, and still I find none. Cut it down! Why should it be wasting the soil?' He replied, 'Sir, let it alone for one more year, until I dig round it and put manure on it. If it bears fruit next year, well and good; but if not, you can cut it down.'" (Luke 13:6–9)

"What can this fig tree mean, if not human nature?...It did not retain the image of God in which it was rooted and nursed...." preached St. Gregory the Great.[1] Although the fig tree appears resplendent with its foliage, it is not fulfilling the reason for its existence. Fig trees are meant to bear fruit. This particular fig tree takes but does not give, takes up room in the orchard and exhausts the soil without giving anything back. The gardener will give it one last chance to produce fruit. If the fig tree does not fulfill its purpose for existing, the orchard owner will have it cut down and removed because it is not fulfilling its destiny.

"Love...does not rejoice in wrongdoing, but rejoices in the truth." (1 Cor 13:6) When we rejoice over our appearance, having a relationship, falling in love, we are feeling good about the foliage of a barren fig tree. The way we look, the existence of a relationship, and the feeling of love are not wrong in and of themselves. However, to celebrate the acquisition of these things as the purpose for our existence is to rejoice over wrongdoing. These things are not the fruits of love. Like the leaves on a fruit tree, they last only for a season. Inevitably they whither, fade, and fall away. Except for a few memories, they leave us with nothing to show for having had them.

The truth about love over which we rejoice is that it is the reason for our existence. Our destiny is to love. We were made for love. We were put on this earth to love. We were born to love. When we do not love, we are like a barren fig tree. All we do is take up space and exhaust the planet's resources without giving anything to anyone. Focusing our time, energy, and interest on our appearances, relationships, and affairs produces nothing that nourishes or sustains anyone.[2] The fruit of love is born out of the sacrifices we make for others, the kindness we show others, and the mercy we offer to others. We cultivate our love for others by keeping the vows and promises of love we gave them. Our love will bear fruit and we will fulfill our destiny when we keep our word that we will always love someone even after our youthful appearance is gone, the relationship is no more, and the falling in love is ended.

The Word of Love
Love...does not rejoice in wrongdoing, but rejoices in the truth. (1 Cor 13:6)

> For if you love those who love you, what reward do you have? Do not even the tax-collectors do the same? And if you greet only your brothers and sisters, what more are you doing than others? Do not even the Gentiles do the same? (Matt 5:46–47)

STORY 11
The Carefree Sower

I have been hurt before: How can I keep from being burned again?

*L*isten! A sower went out to sow. And as he sowed, some seeds fell on the path, and the birds came and ate them up. Other seeds fell on rocky ground, where they did not have much soil, and they sprang up quickly, since they had no depth of soil. But when the sun rose, they were scorched; and since they had no root, they withered away. Other seeds fell among thorns, and the thorns grew up and choked them. Other seeds fell on good soil and brought forth grain, some a hundredfold,

some sixty, some thirty. Let anyone with ears listen!
(Matt 13:3–9)

In the seventh century St. Maximus the Confessor wrote, "Blessed is the man who can love all men equally….He who loves God must of necessity love his neighbor too. And such a man cannot hoard possessions, but so manages them as to please God, giving to each man what he needs. He who bestows alms, imitating God, does not distinguish good from bad, righteous from wicked….He gives alike to all, according to their need."[1] Such a lover is the sower who is unattached in his love of others. He indiscriminately and generously gives to all kinds of ground. He does not pick and choose to attend to some kinds of ground and not others. He can sow with abandon and a carefree spirit because he is not attached to getting a return for his work of love. The sower revels in loving all those he meets.

Many who revel in thinking or feeling that they are in love do not realize that what they are experiencing is not love but attachment. We also do not realize that we can become attached and addicted to anything, including relationships.[2] Jacquelyn Small, a psychotherapist and consultant, states that "we experience pain and suffering whenever our attachment threatens to leave us…attachment is the cause of suffering."[3] When we are attached to having romance, dreams coming true, loving relationships, and a certain person with whom we will live happily ever after, we are out of touch with the reality of life and our capacity to love. When we feel that we cannot be whole without something or a particular someone in our lives we experience suffering and hurt because of our attachment.

To those who are addicted to their feelings and ideas of love, an unattached love is unthinkable. Such love appears to them as "not caring," "cold," and, of course, "unfeeling." Yet, it is this non-attachment to being loved in return that allows the sower the joyous freedom to love all, especially those who are most in need of love. This "non-attachment" explains Small, "does not mean non-caring; it is non-needing...non-obsessing."[4]

Being in love as the sower is, we love those who are like footpaths, beaten down and trampled by the passing crowd. These do not understand how anyone can love them because they do not love themselves. They think of themselves as unlovable and feel unloved. Because they believe what they think and feel above all, they miss the experience of being loved due to the fact that they do not believe that anyone could love them.

Being free to love like the sower, we love those who are like rocky patches of ground with little soil. These are at first overjoyed to be loved by someone. However, love cannot take root in them because they think that love is an emotion. Fear of doing the hard work that love requires reveals what shallow individuals they are. Faced with the heat of what they think are love's unbearable demands, they burn out and the feelings of love quickly wither and wilt.

Being carefree lovers, we love those who can be quite thorny and prickly. Rather than love another selflessly, they concentrate on gratifying the needs they think and feel they have. Attracted by the loveliness of things instead of the loveliness of people, they focus their attention on the acquisition of such things as money, power, feelings, relationships, and self-image. Ironically, by dedicating all their time and energy to such narcissistic pursuits, they succeed only in being emotionally choked to death.

Loving as the sower loves, we will also love without expecting any return from those who are like deep, rich soil. These appreciate being loved. They know both how to receive and how to give love. In being loved, they believe that they are lovable and they love themselves unselfishly. Inspired by the love they have received they, in turn, follow the example of the love they have been given and love the footpaths, the rocky patches of ground, the thorny and prickly people without expecting any return from them. These nonattached lovers multiply the love they have been given a hundred, sixty, and thirtyfold.

Love bears all things—hurt, disappointment, hardship, deception, betrayal, rejection, abandonment, "falling out of love" and more—because love does not believe any of them to be a reason to stop loving someone. Love does not look for return of any kind. Love is not for a reason or for a season. We are in love when we are patient with the person who either does not know how to love or chooses not to love us. We are in love when we are kind to the person who is not interested in us, finds us unattractive, does not care about us, or prefers to love another instead of us. We are in love when we pray for the person who once thought and felt love for us but now no longer does. We are in love when we forgive the person who betrayed, hurt, rejected, deceived, or disappointed us. We are in love when we, like the Master Lover, show mercy with reckless and carefree abandon to all those around us. We are in love when we unite ourselves in an unbreakable bond to the Master Lover. St. Maximus offers these lines from Paul's Letter to the Romans (8:35–39) as "the words of those who attained perfect love":[5]

> Who will separate us from the love of Christ? Will hardship, or distress, or persecution, or famine, or nakedness, or peril, or sword? As it is written, "For your sake we are being killed all day long; we are accounted as sheep to be slaughtered." No, in all these things we are more than conquerors through him who loved us. For I am convinced that neither death, nor life, nor angels, nor rulers, nor things present, nor things to come, nor powers, nor height, nor depth, nor anything else in all creation, will be able to separate us from the love of God in Christ Jesus our Lord. (Rom 8:35–39)

We are the rich soil when we receive the Master's Love and produce a hundred, sixty, and thirty times more love in our world.

The Word of Love
Love...bears all things.... (1 Cor 13:7)

But I say to you, Love your enemies and pray for those who persecute you, so that you may be children of your Father in heaven; for he makes his sun rise on the evil and on the good, and sends rain on the righteous and on the unrighteous. (Matt 5:44–45)

STORY 12
The Gracious Host and the Ungrateful Guests

What kind of lover am I?

*T*hen Jesus said to him, "Someone gave a great dinner and invited many. At the time for the dinner he sent his slave to say to those who had been invited, 'Come; for everything is ready now.' But they all alike began to make excuses. The first said to him, 'I have bought a piece of land, and I must go out and see it; please accept my apologies.' Another said, 'I have bought five yoke of oxen, and I am going to try them out; please accept my apologies.' Another said, 'I have just been married, and therefore I cannot come.' So the *slave returned and reported this to his master. Then the owner of the house became angry and said to his slave, 'Go out at once into the streets and lanes of the town and bring in the poor, the crippled, the blind, and the lame.' And the slave said, 'Sir, what you ordered has been done, and there is still room.' Then the master said to the slave, 'Go out into the roads and lanes, and compel people to come in, so that my house may be filled. For I tell you, none of those who were invited will taste my dinner.'" (Luke 14:16–24)*

In the days the Master Lover told this story, the hosting of a banquet was a great act of love. A great banquet and, especially, a wedding feast were celebrations of love and foreshadowings of the heavenly banquet in the kingdom of love and life in which those who had spent their lives in service to God and neighbor would partake. The host provided everything in the way of food, clothing, and shelter the guests would need for a celebration that could last days. All was freely lavished upon the guests without any expectations of repayment of any kind. To receive an invitation to such a banquet was to be invited to experience love. To decline an invitation to such a magnificent banquet was unheard of: There simply was no reason or excuse not to attend such a feast. No one in his or her right mind would refuse to go or would miss such an occasion of love.

Those who excused themselves from attending the wedding feast would rather pursue their own happiness through possessions than through love. What is of interest to them are things they can claim as their own: a piece of land, five yoke of oxen, a wife. Although they might consider these to be their "loves," in truth, they are not in love. They are attached. Deepak Chopra, a speaker and writer of Eastern spirituality, asserts that "attachment arises whenever [one says], 'I love you because you're mine'...thinks in terms of, 'I,' 'me,' 'mine,'...feel[s] completely attached to another person."[1] The purpose of this kind of connecting with what is "loved" is solely for the gratification of the "lover." Once the property, the car, or the spouse ceases to make the lover happy, they are quickly discarded and replaced with something or someone else.

Love believes all things are good and are to be used for the good of all. The host of the wedding feast generously uses all the things at his disposal for the well-being and happiness of his invited guests without any expectations of seeing a return of any kind. When those he originally invites to the banquet reject his gracious hospitality, he invites others regardless of social standing or ability to repay him. Everyone is welcomed to his table. The host can possess such love because he is not attached to possessions. He does not have the contractual mindset that is a part of many relationships in which one expects certain responses and returns from the other. Those who think and feel that they will find their happiness in attachments and self-gratification cannot understand the host's happiness and passion for loving without any attachment to what he will get in return for his generosity. They will never taste the banquet prepared for those who accept the invitation to be in love. Happiness and fulfillment cannot be found in any thing: not in possessing things, not in doing different things, not in having relationships, not even in getting married. Happiness and fulfillment are experienced by those who use the good things they have for the well-being of others and do not expect any thing in return.

The Word of Love
Love...believes all things.... (1 Cor 13:7)

> He said also to the one who had invited him, "When you give a luncheon or a dinner, do not invite your friends or your brothers or your relatives or rich neighbors, in case they may invite you in return, and you would be repaid. But when you give a banquet, invite the poor, the crippled, the lame, and the blind. And you will be blessed, because they cannot repay you, for you will be repaid at the resurrection of the righteous." One of the dinner guests, on hearing this, said to him, "Blessed is anyone who will eat bread in the kingdom of God!" (Luke 14:12–15)

STORY 13
The Good Shepherd and the Good Lost Sheep

Where and when will I find love?

*N*ow all the tax-collectors and sinners were coming near to listen to him. And the Pharisees and the scribes were grumbling and saying, "This fellow welcomes sinners and eats with them." So he told them this parable: "Which one of you, having a hundred sheep and losing one of them, does not leave the ninety-nine in the wilderness and go after the one that is lost until he finds it? When he has found it, he lays it on his shoulders and *rejoices. And when he comes home, he calls together his friends and neighbors, saying to them, 'Rejoice with me, for I have found my sheep that was lost.' Just so, I tell you, there will be more joy in heaven over one sinner who repents than over ninety-nine righteous people who need no repentance. 'Or what woman having ten silver coins, if she loses one of them, does not light a lamp, sweep the house, and search carefully until she finds it? When she has found it, she calls together her friends and neighbors, saying, "Rejoice with me, for I have found the coin that I had lost." Just so, I tell you, there is joy in the presence of the angels of God over one sinner who repents.'" (Luke 15:1–10)*

The obvious but often overlooked truth of this love story is that the lost sheep does not find the good shepherd. The good shepherd finds the lost sheep. So it is with love. We do not find love. Love finds us. When we put all our hope in what we know or feel to tell us where love can be found, we are lost sheep. Foolishly, we think we can find love by following or listening to our feelings. Like a dog chasing its tail, we run around in circles vainly trying to catch the certain positive feelings of love while trying to avoid or to get rid of the negative feelings we dislike and think do us harm. Insanely, we repeat the same opinions, behaviors, patterns in our relationships, ways of responding and reacting to others, all in the dysfunctional thinking that this time things will be different. With nothing more to hope in than ourselves, we get stuck in a vicious and never ending cycle of "if only's." If only we could find someone who loves us, everything would be all right. If only we could become someone's one-and-only, we would feel affirmed and worthwhile. If only our dream of living happily ever after would come true, all would be well. Trusting only our feelings in our search for love ultimately will get us hopelessly lost and leave us feeling more unloved than ever before. Believing our opinions and what the dominant culture's media tells us about love will lull us into a deep sleep until that moment when we awake up to find ourselves in a nightmare, lost, alone, and unloved.

We will always be lost in regard to love as long as we think that it is up to *us* to find love. In order to be found *by* love, we must be good lost sheep. We must dispose ourselves to being encountered by love by putting all our hope in love and in nothing else. As good lost sheep, we do not put any hope in change, in the future, or in our dreams coming true. To hope in love means to believe that the Good Shepherd "has loved us first and he continues to do so" (*DCE* 17). We trust in the Good Shepherd's word of love to us. Even in spite of what we might think or feel, we believe that we are loved. Because we are first and always loved by the Master Lover, "we too, then, can respond with love" (*DCE* 17), no matter what the situation. In the joyful assurance that all things are well, we good lost sheep wait and watch patiently for Love to find us. While we wait and watch in joyful hope for the day that the Good Shepherd will find us and carry us home to eternal life with him, we cheerfully dedicate ourselves to doing works of mercy and charity for the rest of his flock.

The Word of Love
Love...hopes all things.... (1 Cor 13:7)

> See that none of you repays evil for evil, but always seek to do good to one another and to all. Rejoice always, pray without ceasing, give thanks in all circumstances; for this is the will of God in Christ Jesus for you. (1 Thes 5:15–18)

STORY 14
The Buried Treasure

What is the price of love?

The kingdom of heaven is like treasure hidden in a field, which someone found and hid; then in his joy he goes and sells all that he has and buys that field. Again, the kingdom of heaven is like a merchant in search of fine pearls; on finding one pearl of great value, he went and sold all that he had and bought it. (Matt 13:44–46)

Love is the treasure that is buried in every one of us. The price of uncovering it and realizing its worth is the sum total of all we possess. Because being in love far and away exceeds the sum of all the things we have, the selling of everything we have in order to love is the bargain of a lifetime. "Love now becomes concern and care for the other. No longer is it self-seeking, a sinking in the intoxication of happiness; instead it seeks the good of the beloved: It becomes renunciation and it is ready and even willing for sacrifice" (*DCE* 6).

Love is a pearl of great value. To be in love is worth every penny we have. Nothing in this world is its equal. Nothing can substitute for having love. Without love we have nothing. Without love we do nothing. Without love we are nothing. No matter what we feel, know, or possess, we have nothing if we do not have love.

Not being able to offer us genuine love, the dominant culture would have us think that we can have love at a price that we can afford. The marketplace is all too eager to sell us something to which we can attach our illusions of love: dream vacations, romantic getaways, "loving" relationships, sex outside of marriage, intimate affairs. These cheap imitations of love that pass for the real thing in our society cannot stand the test of time. They simply cannot and do not last. Perhaps, this is one of the reasons why we are afraid of committing ourselves to a life of genuine love. Because it has been our repeated experience that nothing is forever except diamonds, we always want to keep something in reserve to purchase the next new substitute for love when the old one has lost its glitter or ceases to be.

Love endures all things as finite and, therefore, as incapable of making us happy, secure, and fulfilled.

The price of making the treasure of love buried within each of us our own is the faithful giving of ourselves to others. This is accomplished through the giving of our word of love to others and keeping our word to always love those we have promised. Spending ourselves and our lives in loving service to those to whom we have committed ourselves is something we cannot afford not to do. An ancient Chinese proverb puts it this way: "If you want to be happy for an hour, take a nap. If you want to be happy for a day, attend a sumptuous banquet. If you want to be happy for a week, go fishing. If you want to be happy for a month, get married. However, if you want to be happy the rest of your life, spend your whole life serving others."

Spending our whole life keeping our commitments, promises, and vows of love is to have found a pearl of great value.

The Word of Love

> If I speak in the tongues of mortals and of angels, but do not have love, I am a noisy gong or a clanging cymbal. And if I have prophetic powers, and understand all mysteries and all knowledge, and if I have all faith, so as to remove mountains, but do not have love, I am nothing. If I give away all my possessions, and if I hand over my body so that I may

boast, but do not have love, I gain nothing. (1 Cor 13:1–3)

No one has greater love than this, to lay down one's life for one's friends. (John 15:13)

The Master Lover and the Fearful, Lazy Apprentice

Is it better to have loved and lost than to have never loved at all?

*F*or it is as if a man, going on a journey, summoned his slaves and entrusted his property to them; to one he gave five talents, to another two, to another one, to each according to his ability. Then he went away. The one who had received the five talents went off at once and traded with them, and made five more talents. In the same way, the one who had the two talents made two more talents. But the one who had received the one talent went off and dug a hole in the ground and hid his master's money. After a long time the master of those slaves came and settled accounts with them. Then the one who had received the five talents came forward, bringing five more talents, saying, "Master, you handed over to me five talents; see, I have made five more talents." His master said to him, "Well done, good and trustworthy slave; you have been trustworthy in a few things, I will put you in charge of many things; enter into the joy of your master." And the one with the two talents also came forward, saying, "Master, you handed over to me two talents; see, I have made two more talents." His master said to him, "Well done, good and trustworthy slave; you have been trustworthy in a few things, I will put you in charge of many things; enter into the joy of your master." Then the one who had received the one talent also came forward, saying, "Master, I knew that you were a harsh man, reaping where you did not sow, and gathering where you did not scatter seed; so I was afraid, and I went and hid your talent in the ground. Here you have what is yours." But his master replied, "You wicked and lazy slave! You knew, did you, that I reap where I did not sow, and gather where I did not scatter? Then you ought to have invested my money with the bankers, and on my return I would have received *what was my own with interest. So take the talent from him, and give it to the one with the ten talents. For to all those who have, more will be given, and they will have an abundance; but from those who have nothing, even what they have will be taken away. As for this worthless slave, throw him into the outer darkness, where there will be weeping and gnashing of teeth." (Matt 25:14–30)*

"Love can be 'commanded' because it has first been given" (*DCE* 14). While we may differ individually as to the number and kinds of talents we possess, the one talent we all have is the ability to love. Making use of that talent, however, is risky business. When we love we put ourselves, our lives, and our feelings at risk. When we love we open ourselves to the possibility of having our hearts broken, our lives ruined, and our feelings hurt.

Love is not only risky, it is hard work. Love is hard work because love never ends (1 Cor 13:8). It is hard work to never cease being faithful to those we promised our love. Wayne Dyer, a noted speaker and author, states that "the true test of love is loving those who refuse to return it as [we] would prefer."[1] When we think of love as an investment and are faced with "losing" what we prefer not to, we grow afraid. When we actually experience a loss, we are apt to withdraw from ever taking any more risks with love.

The slave whom the Master Lover instructs in the ways of love is afraid of losing the only talent he was given. Afraid of giving himself to loving, the slave thinks that he can live life without commitments and responsibilities. Although the slave would say that he believes in love, he does not. Because he believes that everything, even love, comes to an end, he is not about to risk himself in a venture that is doomed to fail. To his way of thinking love comes naturally, meaning that love is spontaneous, effortless, and easy. Deep down the slave is afraid of the risk and the hard work that love entails. This fear of his makes him lazy and, therefore, "wicked" and "worthless." He thinks that he can avoid loss and save himself by burying the talent he has to love. However, by not committing to love, he unwittingly commits to fear and nonlove. In the end the slave fails to save himself. A slave to his fears and feelings, he experiences what he feared most, namely, a life lived in "outer darkness" of alienation and isolation that is aptly described in the story as the "weeping and gnashing of teeth."

Being afraid of risking ourselves in love and of doing the hard work of love always fails. We cannot save ourselves by burying our talent to love. The dominant culture would have us believe that we can save ourselves by avoiding commitments of love. In reality, when we do not commit ourselves to the risks and hard work of love, we commit to fear and nonlove. This is slavery of the worst kind. Acting out of a fear of losing something or someone, of being hurt and of having our hearts broken only assures us of a "wicked" outcome. "Fear is useless" (Mark 5:36)[2] because fear always fails us. Fear is a self-fulfilling prophecy. The more we listen to our fears and try to preserve or protect ourselves from further hurt and suffering, the more we will experience our lives as dark and loveless. Being in love is believing in the power of love to mend our hearts, heal our wounds, and experience life as worth living. Being in love is being unafraid to risk ourselves and all our resources for the sake of others. The hardest work we will ever do is to keep on loving when we are faced with losing everything. Being in love is not being afraid to do the hard work of remaining faithful to the promises of love that we have given to others. Because "love never ends" (1 Cor 13:8), ultimately, we cannot lose. Even if we have loved and lost, those who have learned from the Master Lover how to love go right on loving no matter what the cost. For in the end there is no end for those who love.

The Word of Love
Love never ends. (1 Cor 13:8)

> There is no fear in love, but perfect love casts out fear; for fear has to do with punishment, and whoever fears has not reached perfection in love. (1 John 4:18)

Conclusion: To Be in Love

"When Jesus speaks in his parables….these are no mere words: They constitute an explanation of his very being and activity": in contemplating love as manifested in Jesus and in his love stories, we discover "the path along which [our] life and love must move" (DCE 12). Life is not about being successful or knowledgeable or always being on the winning side. Life is about being in love. In the twelfth chapter of the Gospel of Mark a student of the law approached the Master Lover and asked him questions about life and love to which he already knew the answers. The Master was impressed with his

knowledge of the truth but remarked that his knowl-
edge was worthless as long as he remained outside
the kingdom of love by not living in love. Richard
Rohr, OFM, in commenting on what the Master
Lover told the young man, asserts: "We do not think
ourselves into a new way of living. We live ourselves
into a new way of thinking." [1]

The reader was counseled in the Introduction of
this book to relinquish false assumptions and old ways of
thinking in order to become free to live and to think in
another way. Those false assumptions included the
notion that mere human words possess power and that
generating and growing a "relationship" suffices for loving. The basic premise of this book and the foundational
principle of the "new way of thinking" is that the conviction that each of us is already born into God's loving relationship. Walter D. Ray affirms: "We are not seeking a
relationship; we are in relationship....[and] to be in relationship we must *be* in the relationship." [2] As love
embraces us, we must embrace love.

The passionate love that God has for human
beings is reflected in the Hebrew scriptures, especially in
God's love song:

> Arise, my love, my fair one, and come
> away; for now the winter is past, the rain
> is over and gone. The flowers appear on
> the earth; the time of singing has come,

and the voice of the turtledove is heard in our land. The fig tree puts forth its figs, and the vines are in blossom; they give forth fragrance. Arise, my love, my fair one, and come away. (Song of Songs 2:10–13; see *DCE* 10)

In *DCE* 17, Pope Benedict XVI provides us with an illustration of how, in the New Testament, Jesus-God exemplifies the depth of that love:

> God loved us first, says the Letter of John (cf. 4:10), and this love of God has appeared in our midst. He has become visible in as much as he "has sent his only Son into the world, so that we might live through him" (1 John 4:9). God has made himself visible: in Jesus we are able to see the Father (cf. John 14:9). Indeed, God is visible in a number of ways. In the love-story recounted by the Bible, he comes towards us, he seeks to win our hearts, all the way to the Last Supper, to the piercing of his heart on the Cross, to his appearances after the Resurrection and to the great deeds by which, through the activity of the Apostles, he guided the nascent Church along its path. Nor has the Lord been absent from subsequent Church history:

he encounters us ever anew, in the men and women who reflect his presence, in his word, in the sacraments, and especially in the Eucharist. In the Church's Liturgy, in her prayer, in the living community of believers, we experience the love of God, we perceive his presence and we thus learn to recognize that presence in our daily lives. He has loved us first and he continues to do so; we too, then, can respond with love. God does not demand of us a feeling which we ourselves are incapable of producing. He loves us, he makes us see and experience his love, and since he has "loved us first," love can also blossom as a response within us.... The love-story between God and man consists in the very fact that this communion of will increases in a communion of thought and sentiment, and thus our will and God's will increasingly coincide: God's will is no longer for me an alien will, something imposed on me from without by the commandments, but it is now my own will, based on the realization that God is in fact more deeply present to me than I am to myself. Then self-abandonment to God increases and God becomes our joy (cf. Ps 73:23–28).

Henri J. M. Nouwen, a noted author of more than thirty books on Christian spirituality, writes: "All human relationships, be they between parents and children, husbands and wives, lovers and friends, or between members of a community, are meant to be signs of God's love for humanity as a whole and each person in particular."[3] A characteristic of relationships is that they have more to do with God and faithful love than they do with our power to create, make, grow, or strengthen them. "When we live as if human relationships are 'human-made' and therefore subject to the shifting and changing of human regulations and customs, we cannot expect anything but the immense fragmentation and alienation that characterize our society."[4]

Through the way he lived his life and the telling of his love stories, the Master Lover teaches us how to be in love and how to communicate that love. For Jesus, love does consist of sharing but not the sharing of feelings, ideas, and individual stories. Jesus' love stories teach us that love is communicated by the sharing of our bread, our belief in the power of love, and the peace of being in love. We communicate love by sharing our bread with those who are hungry, our clothing with those who are naked, and our shelter with those who are homeless. We love others regardless of how we feel or what we think about them because they are our neighbors, our sisters and brothers, with whom love has already put us in relationship.

For those who are or who consider themselves to be victims, wounded and unloved, we share our belief in the power of love to heal, reconcile, unite, and protect us from lasting harm and unhappiness. Love has power that words do not. That is why the Master Lover urges us to "love, not in word or speech, but in truth and action." (1 John 3:18). Love moves us far beyond where our feelings and thinking will allow us to go. Believing in the power of love instead of the power of words gets us over and beyond everything that happened in the past and over which we are "sick." Believing in the power of love instead of the power of words liberates us from the prison of our fears and anxieties about the future. It is love and not words that has the power to heal all our wounds, free us from all our worries, and give us a new life of peace and joy. It is in this love that we were created to abide; it is about this love that the author of 1 John 4:16–21 instructs: "God is love, and those who abide in love abide in God, and God abides in them....Those who say, 'I love God,' and hate their brothers or sisters, are liars; for those who do not love a brother or sister whom they have seen, cannot love God whom they have not seen. The commandment we have from him is this: those who love God must love their brothers and sisters also."

Those who feel themselves sorely tried and unjustly dealt with should be considered to be the subjects of a special call to abide in faith-based love. In *DCE* 38, Pope Benedict invites us to contemplate:

> Certainly Job could complain before God about the presence of incomprehensible and apparently unjustified suf-

fering in the world. In his pain he cried out: "Oh, that I knew where I might find him, that I might come even to his seat!...I would learn what he would answer me, and understand what he would say to me. Would he contend with me in the greatness of his power?... Therefore I am terrified at his presence; when I consider, I am in dread of him. God has made my heart faint; the Almighty has terrified me" (23:3, 5–6, 15–16). Often we cannot understand why God refrains from intervening. Yet he does not prevent us from crying out, like Jesus on the Cross: "My God, my God, why have you forsaken me?" (Matt 27:46). We should continue asking this question in prayerful dialogue before his face: "Lord, holy and true, how long will it be?" (Rev 6:10). It is Saint Augustine who gives us faith's answer to our sufferings: *"Si comprehendis, non est Deus"*—"if you understand him, he is not God." Our protest is not meant to challenge God, or to suggest that error, weakness or indifference can be found in him. For the believer, it is impossible to imagine that God is powerless or that "perhaps he is asleep" (cf. 1 Kgs 18:27). Instead, our crying out is, as it was for Jesus on the

Cross, the deepest and most radical way of affirming our faith in his sovereign power. Even in their bewilderment and failure to understand the world around them, Christians continue to believe in the "goodness and loving kindness of God" (Titus 3:4). Immersed like everyone else in the dramatic complexity of historical events, they remain unshakably certain that God is our Father and loves us, even when his silence remains incomprehensible.

With everyone we meet we share the peace of being in love. Jesus gives us peace but "not as the world gives" peace. (John 14:27) The peace that the Master Lover gives us is the result of being in love. This peace comes from our faith that we are loved and already in a relationship with everyone we meet, from our hope that we are in love's providential care, and from our love that goes beyond feelings and the world's understanding of justice and forgives others of whatever offense or infidelity they may have committed. A little story about St. Silouan the Athonite illustrates well the significant difference between Jesus' forgiving love and our self-righteous, judgmental perception that justice is somehow served by the death and eternal punishment of the sinner:

A hermit proclaimed with evident satisfaction that "God will punish all atheists.

They will burn in everlasting fire."
Obviously upset, Silouan asked the hermit, "Tell me, supposing you went to paradise, and there you looked down and saw someone burning in hell-fire, would you feel happy?" "It can't be helped. It would be their own fault," replied the hermit. Silouan answered him in a sorrowful countenance. "Love could not bear that," he said. "We must pray for all."[5]

Jesus' love stories communicated the "how" of God's love just as his miracles witnessed to the power of that love. Jesus' love stories are but one Word, his promise, to faithfully love us without conditions or limitations and with all his heart, soul, mind, and strength.[6] The following poem is our own interpretation of Jesus' promise to love us:

> I promise you, my Bride, to always be
> patient.
> Even if I should feel impatient, I will
> never act out emotionally.
> I will always act patiently
> and will wait longingly for you.
>
> I promise you, beautiful one,
> to always be kind.
> In spite of what I might think of you, I

will always treat you and everyone I
meet with kindness and tender care.

I promise you, salt of the earth,
to never be envious.
I will never envy anything or anyone
more than you. Your good and your
well-being are my greatest concern.

I promise you, bone of my bone,
never to be boastful.
I will never boast about myself
to others or to you at your expense.
Rather, I will tell everyone how good
and beautiful a person you are
and how blessed we are that you are.

I promise you, flesh of my flesh,
never to be arrogant.
I will never put you down in public or in
private.
I will always respect and honor you all
the days of my life.

I promise you, my daughter/my son,
never to be rude.
I will never hold anything against you,
never blame you for any of my unhappiness and never mistreat you in any
way.

I promise you, light of the world,
never to be jealous of you or of anyone.
I will not insist on doing things my way
or having my desires met before yours.

I promise you, blessed one,
never to be irritable.
I will never act out of anger against you
or anyone else.
I will control all my emotions and pas-
sions with the use of reason and will
never allow them to harden into bit-
terness or hatred.

I promise you, cherished one,
never to be resentful.
I will not dwell on the past or on hurts
and misunderstandings.
Before sunset I will ask for your forgiveness for what I have done wrong and
forgive you if you have wronged me.

I promise you, precious one,
never to rejoice over wrongdoing but
rejoice with the truth.
I will never gloat over your mistakes or
accuse you of wrongdoing.
I will never compete with you in a con-
test of who is right and who is wrong.

Rather I will rejoice in the truth that sets
    both of us free
to love more deeply and completely.

I promise you, my sister/my brother,
to bear all things,
trials, tribulations, setbacks,
and disappointments in the name of love.

I promise you, dearest,
to believe all things
will work for our benefit
because we have as our God
the One who is Love, Compassion, and
    Mercy.

I promise you, friend,
to hope all things
are well and will be well.
I will not listen to my fears and anxieties
    but will put my trust and hope
in the power of love to make all things
    right.

I promise you, treasured one,
to endure all things.
Come what may,
I will always be faithful to you in good
    times and in hard times, in sickness
    and in health.

I promise you, beloved,
to love you without fail and without end.

"We know love by this, that [Jesus] laid down his life for us—and we ought to lay down our lives for one another" (1 John 3:16). Through his love stories Jesus teaches us that true love consists of this: the giving of ourselves and our lives to those we meet each and every day by keeping our promise to love them by sharing with them our bread, our belief in the power of love, and our peace of being in love. Because we are loved by the Master Lover, have the promise of his undying love, and are born with the capacity to love, we can be in love beginning now and continuing forever. A more joyful or happier ending to our love stories there could not be.

Notes

Prologue

1. *Catechism of the Catholic Church*, *2nd ed.* (Liberia Editrice Vaticana, through the United States Catholic Conference, Washington, DC: 1997), 404.

2. David Brooks, "All Cultures Are Not Equal," *New York Times*, (August 10, 2005), A23.

3. Pope John Paul II, *Ut Unum Sint* (That They May Be One), May 25, 1995. No. 54.

Introduction

1. Bishop Kallistos of Diokleia, "The Use of the Jesus Prayer in Daily Life," *Eastern Churches Journal* 7, no. 30 (2000): 17.

2. Walter Burghardt, *Preaching: The Art and the Craft* (Mahwah, NJ: Paulist Press, 1987), 197.

3. M. Scott Peck, *The Road Less Traveled* (New York: Simon and Shuster, 1978), 116–17.

4. See *Catechism of the Catholic Church*, 2nd ed. (New York: Doubleday, 2000), part two, chapter two: "The Sacramental Celebration of the Paschal Mystery," article 1, "Celebrating the Church's Liturgy," numbers 1145–62: 296, and following. It may be noted here that eminent liturgist Robert Taft, SJ, characterizes ritual communication as "a set of conventions, an organized pattern of signs and gestures which the members use to interpret and enact for themselves, and to express and transmit to others, their relation to reality." Thus the community is enabled to relate effectively to the present and cope with the future. In the process of ritual representation, past constitutive events are made present in ritual time, in order to communicate their force to new generations of the social group, providing a continuity of identity throughout history. Taft then makes the distinction between natural and liturgical ritualizing. Natural attempts to contact the divine, to mediate to present beings the power of God's intervention in past saving events. With Christian liturgical ritual, it is the other way around. It is the worship of the already saved, the celebration of how God has touched us, has united us to himself and is ever present to us and dwelling in us. It is a participation in the eternally present salvific Pasch of Christ ("Thanksgiving for the Light: Towards a Theology of Vespers," *Diakonia* 13, 1978: 27–50).

5. Pope John Paul II, *Fides et Ratio* (Faith and Reason), September 14, 1998: 32.

6. Dave Barry, *Dave Barry's Complete Guide to Guys* (New York: Random House, 1995), p. 65.

Story 1

1. Vladimir Berzonsky, *The Gift of Love* (Crestwood, NY: St. Vladimir's Seminary Press, 1985), 75.

Story 3

1. St. Basil the Great, *Detailed Rules for Monks*, Resp. 2, 1:PG 31, 908–10. From the second reading of the Office of Readings for Tuesday of the first week in Ordinary Time. *The Liturgy of the Hours According to the Roman Rite: Ordinary Time, Weeks 1–17*, Volume III (New York: Catholic Book Publishing Company, 1975), 59.

Story 5

1. Archbishop Anthony Bloom, *Meditations: A Spiritual Journey through the Parables* (Danville, NJ: Dimension Books, 1971), 41.

2. Deepak Chopra, *The Way of the Wizard* (New York: Harmony Books, 1995), 107.

Story 7

1. *Fides et Ratio*, 32.

Story 8

1. Richard Carlson, *Don't Sweat the Small Stuff—and It's All Small Stuff* (New York: Hyperion, 1997), 33–35.

2. Cf. 1 John 4:19–21.

Story 9

1. Cf. Point 7, "Forgive," Emrika Padus, ed., *The Complete Guide to Your Emotions and Your Health* (New York: Rodale Press, 1992), 85.

2. *New American Bible*, Saint Joseph edition (New York: Catholic Book Publishing, 1970), 207.

Story 10

1. St. Gregory the Great, *Parables of the Gospel*, Homily XXXI, excerpted in *The Bible and the Holy Fathers for Orthodox*, Johanna Manley, ed. (Menlo Park, CA: Monastery Books, 1990), 552.

2. Thomas Hopko, *All the Fullness of God* (Crestwood, NY: St. Vladimir's Seminary Press, 1982), 183–84.

Story 11

1. E. Kadloubovsky and G. E. H. Palmer, translators, *Early Fathers from the Philokalia* (London: Faber and Faber, 1973): 288–89.

2. "An individual can also become addicted to relationships or patterns of relationships, at times sexu-

ally, in a manner that is socially unacceptable. Such addiction to a relationship with persons alters the addict's life to the degree that it destroys all other relationships. In additive love relationships another person becomes needed in such an absorbing way, often to the point of survival, that perception and judgment become impaired. In such addictions there is: a loss of personal autonomy and self-worth; a failure to maintain other interests and relationships integrated with the relationship; jealousy and possessiveness; a lack of friendship between the lovers" (J. G. Schner, SJ, "Addictions" in *Psychology, Counseling and the Seminarian*, Robert Wisner ed. [Washington, DC: National Catholic Educational Association Seminary Department, 1993]:29).

3. Quoted in Emrika Padus, ed., *The Complete Guide to Your Emotions and Your Health*, 275.

4. Ibid.

5. Kadloubovsky and Palmer, *Early Fathers from the Philokalia*, 295.

Story 12

1. Deepak Chopra, *The Way of the Wizard* (New York: Harmony Books, 1995), 104.

Story 15

1. Wayne Dyer, *Gifts from Eykis* (New York: Pocket Books, 1983); 21.

2. *New American Bible*, 49.

Conclusion: To Be in Love

1. Richard Rohr, *Everything Belongs: The Gift of Contemplative Prayer* (New York: The Crossroad Publishing Co., 2003), 19.

2. Book Review, "'Eastern Orthodoxy through Western Eyes' through Eastern Eyes: An Eastern Reflection on Donald Fairbairn's *Eastern Orthodoxy through Western Eyes*" (Louisville/London: Westminster John Knox Press, 2002; reviewed by Walter D. Ray in *Religion in Eastern Europe*, XXIV, 4 (August 2004), 49.

3. Henri J. M. Nouwen, *Here and Now: Living in the Spirit* (New York: The Crossroad Publishing Co., 1994), 127.

4. Ibid., 128.

5. Sophrony, Archimandrite, *The Monk of Mount Athos: Staretz Silouan, 1866-1938,* trans. Rosemary Edmonds (London: Mowbrays, 1973), 32.

6. Mark 12:30.

Annotated Recommended Readings

Pope Benedict XVI. *Deus Caritas Est* (God Is Love) (Washington, DC: United States Conference of Catholic Bishops, 2006).

  The first part of Pope Benedict's first encyclical clarifies "essential facts concerning the love which God mysteriously and gratuitously offers to man, together with the intrinsic link between that love and…Human love." The more-concrete second part treats the ecclesial exercise of the commandment of love of neighbor.

Blommestijn, Hein, Jos Huls, and Kess Waaijman. *The Footprints of Love: John of the Cross as Guide in the Wilderness* (Leuven, Belgium: Peeters, 2000).

  An introduction to Carmelite spirituality and an exploration of the logic of transformational divine love: God withdraws himself so that human life may take shape as "a trail made up of the footprints of love." Four of John's great commentaries and one of his poems are subjected to study.

Catechism of the Catholic Church, 2nd ed. (Vatican City: Libreria Editrice Vaticana, 1997).

A systematic articulation of faith and doctrine, complete with index, footnotes, and cross references for further study. Of special interest is the material on charity as a theological virtue.

Dubay, Thomas. *Fire Within: St. Teresa of Avila, St. John of the Cross, and the Gospel—on Prayer* (San Francisco: Ignatius Press, 1989).

A synthesis of the teachings of two great doctors of the church arising from the gospel imperative of personal prayer and the call to holiness.

Evdokimoff, Paul Nikolaevich. *The Sacrament of Love: The Nuptial Mystery in the Light of the Orthodox Tradition* (Crestwood, NY: St. Vladimir's Seminary Press, 1985).

A deeply theological reflection not only on marriage in the image of God in the trinitarian communion of divine persons, but also on love as the basis of monastic and nonmonastic celibacy.

Forest, Jim. *The Ladder of the Beatitudes* (Maryknoll, NY: Orbis Books, 1999).

An easily approachable work treating the various aspects of a life in loving communion with God that begins with the quote from St. John Climacus, "Blessed is the person whose desire for God has become like the lover's passion for the beloved."

Glavich, Mary Kathleen, SND. *Called to Love: Your Christian Vocation* (Notre Dame, IN: Ave Maria Press, 2000).

A guidebook for teens for discerning a particular way in which to live out one's baptismal identity in the image of Christ who loves. Discussion questions and selected vocabulary lists are included.

Jalics, Franz. *Contemplative Retreat: An Introduction to the Contemplative Way of Life and to the Jesus Prayer* (Munchen, Germany: Xulon Press, 2003).

A ten-step guide based on the author's personal life, spiritual growth, and extensive pastoral experience that leads to immediate awareness of the reality of God's presence. This book can be used as a handbook for a closed retreat or for a retreat in everyday life.

Pope John Paul II. *Veritatis Splendor* (The Splendor of Truth), August 6, 1993.

Available on the Vatican's Encyclicals/ Documents web site. A reaffirmation of the fundamentals of the church's moral teaching, "fundamentals that can be found only in God."

Kadloubovsky, E., and G. E. H. Palmer, translators. *Early Fathers from the Philokalia* (London: Faber and Faber, 1973).

Selections of writings that remain relevant for those who seek to live the principles of the Christian tradition that encompasses not only space but time as well.

Laranaga, Ignacio. *Sensing Your Hidden Presence: Toward Intimacy with God* (Sherbrooke, QC, Canada: Editions Paulines, 1992).

The author lends his effort to "picking up" the word God in our secularized world and attempts "to express the ultimate mystery of God, that God is love itself, the infinite irradiation of love, the unfathomable dynamic of loving, the genesis and consummation of everything that can be called love" (from the Preface to the English edition).

Lewis, Clive Staples. *The Four Loves* (New York: Harcourt, Brace, 1960).

This exploration of the four basic kinds of human love—affection, friendship, erotic love, and the love of God—has achieved the status of being a modern classic on the subject of love.

Murphy-O'Connor, Jerome. *Becoming Human Together: The Pastoral Anthropology of St. Paul* (Wilmington, DE: Michael Glazier, Inc., 1982).

An exposition of Paul's theological anthropology that leads to insights into inauthentic versus authentic existence in the body of Christ, the locus of true Christian community of which freedom is the primordial characteristic.

Nouwen, Henri J. M. *Here and Now: Living in the Spirit* (New York: The Crossroad Publishing Co., 1994).

Meditations that result in practical instruction in living in a world in which "love is so ambiguous." A major lesson is that God is much closer to us than we usually realize.

Rohr, Richard. *Everything Belongs: The Gift of Contemplative Prayer* (New York: The Crossroad Publishing Co., 2003).

This book is an introduction and guide to "what it means to be contemplative." A personal retreat guide for those who hunger for a deeper prayer life but don't know what contemplation truly is. Complete with reflection guide.

Works Cited

Barry, Dave. *Dave Barry's Complete Guide to Guys.* New York: Random House, 1995.

St. Basil the Great, *Detailed Rules for Monks,* Resp. 2, 1:PG 31, 908–10. From the second reading of the Office of Readings for Tuesday of the first week in Ordinary Time. *The Liturgy of the Hours According to the Roman Rite: Ordinary Time, Weeks 1–17,* Volume III. New York: Catholic Book Publishing Company, 1975.

Berzonsky, Vladimir. *The Gift of Love.* Crestwood, NY: St. Vladimir's Seminary Press, 1985.

Bloom, Archbishop Anthony. *Meditations: A Spiritual Journey through the Parables.* Danville, NJ: Dimension Books, 1971.

Book Review. "'Eastern Orthodoxy through Western Eyes' through Eastern Eyes: An Eastern Reflection on Donald Fairbairn's *Eastern Orthodoxy through Western Eyes*" (Louisville/London: Westminster John Knox Press, 2002); reviewed by Walter D. Ray in *Religion in Eastern Europe*, XXIV, No. 4 (August 2004): 47–55.

Burghardt, Walter. *Preaching: The Art and the Craft*. Mahwah, NJ: Paulist Press, 1987.

Carlson, Richard. *Don't Sweat the Small Stuff—and It's All Small Stuff*. New York: Hyperion, 1997.

Catechism of the Catholic Church, 2nd ed. Vatican City: Liberia Editrice Vaticana, 1997.

Dyer, Wayne. *Gifts from Eykis*. New York: Pocket Books, 1983.

Hopko, Thomas. *All the Fullness of God*. Crestwood, NY: St. Vladimir's Seminary Press, 1982.

Pope John Paul II. *Fides et Ratio* (Faith and Reason), September 14, 1998.

Kadloubovsky, E. and G. E. H. Palmer, translators. *Early Fathers from the Philokalia*. London: Faber and Faber, 1973.

Manley, Johanna, ed. *The Bible and the Holy Fathers for Orthodox*. Menlo Park, CA: Monastery Books, 1990.

New American Bible. Saint Joseph edition. New York: Catholic Book Publishing, 1970.

Nouwen, Henri J. M. *Here and Now: Living in the Spirit*. New York: The Crossroad Publishing Co., 1994.

Peck, M. Scott. *The Road Less Traveled*. New York: Simon and Shuster, 1978.

Rohr, Richard. *Everything Belongs: The Gift of Contemplative Prayer*. New York: The Crossroad Publishing Co., 2003.

Schner, J. G., SJ. "Addictions," in *Psychology, Counseling and the Seminarian*, Robert Wisner, ed. Washington, DC: National Catholic Educational Association Seminary Department, 1993; 25–41.

Sophrony, Archimandrite, *The Monk of Mount Athos: Staretz Silouan, 1866-1938*, trans. Rosemary Edmonds. London: Mowbrays, 1973.

Taft, Robert, SJ. "Thanksgiving for the Light: Towards a Theology of Vespers," *Diakonia* 13 (1978): 27–50.

ILLUMINATIONBOOKS

Other Books in the Series

The Mysteries of Light
> by Roland J. Faley, TOR

Healing Mysteries
> by Adrian Gibbons Koester

Carrying the Cross with Christ
> by Joseph T. Sullivan

Saintly Deacons
> by Deacon Owen F. Cumming

Finding God Today
> by E. Springs Steele

Hail Mary and Rhythmic Breathing
> by Richard Galentino

The Eucharist
> by Joseph M. Champlin

Gently Grieving
> by Constance M. Mucha

Devotions for Caregivers
> by Marilyn Driscoll

Be a Blessing
> by Elizabeth M. Nagel

The Art of Affirmation
> by Robert Furey